Tsunami!
Deadly Wall of Water
Revised Edition

by Jeff Putnam

Reading Consultant:
Timothy Rasinski, Ph.D.
Professor of Reading Education
Kent State University

Content Consultant:
Tad Murty
Vice President
International Tsunami Society,
Department of Civil Engineering
University of Ottawa

CAPSTONE PRESS
a capstone imprint

Published by Red Brick™ Learning
1710 Roe Crest Drive, North Mankato, Minnesota 56003.
www.mycapstone.com

Library of Congress Cataloging-in-Publication Data is available on the Library of Congress website.
  ISBN: 978-1-5157-4432-0 (paperback)

Created by Kent Publishing Services, Inc.
Designed by Signature Design Group, Inc.
Edited by Jerry Ruff, Managing Editor, Red Brick™ Learning
Red Brick™ Learning Editorial Director: Mary Lindeen

Table of Contents

People enjoy a day at the beach.

— CHAPTER **1** —

The Sea Turns Deadly

It is the day after Christmas—December 26, 2004.

*You are a **tourist** at a seaside resort in Asia.*

The ocean is calm. The beach is busy.

Children are swimming with their parents.

An Ordinary Day?

You walk along the crowded beach. The sun warms your skin. Palm trees wave softly. Fishermen load their nets onto boats. You watch children playing in the water. You hear their happy shouts.

Then you hear a new, odd sound. It sounds almost like a lion roaring. "What could it be?" you wonder.

---

tourist (TOOR-ist): someone who travels for pleasure

Is There Something Out There?

People around you are pointing out to sea. "What are they looking at?" you ask a woman. "Is there something out there?"

Yes, there is something out there. It is a wall of white, foamy water. It is a mile out. It seems to be moving fast—very fast.

Suddenly, a fisherman next to you drops his net. He screams.

"Run!" he yells. "Run for your life!"

His next word makes the hair on your neck stand up.

"Tsunami!" (soo-NAH-mee)

People watch as the 2004 Indian Ocean tsunami makes its way to shore. Many people did not understand what was happening.

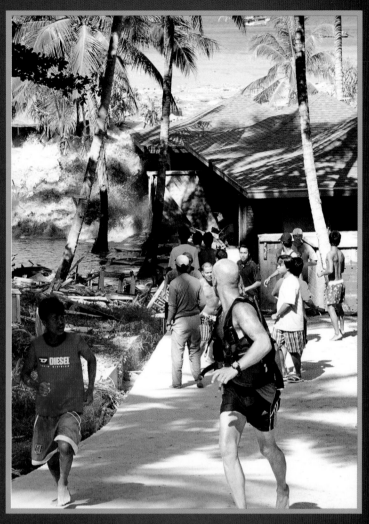

Local people and tourists run from the beaches as waves crash into shore. Many died in the 2004 Indian Ocean tsunami.

Looking for Safety

All around you, people run for their lives. Men and women carry babies and small children. They run away from the sea and toward the town. They're running to higher ground—anywhere that might be safe.

The sound of the tsunami grows louder. So do the screams of the people **fleeing** the beach.

Terror from the Sea

You are running now, too. People bump you as they run. You fall down. A mother stops to pick up a baby. A young man carries an older man. Everyone is running away from the oncoming water.

"Where will I go?" you ask yourself. "Where will I be safe?"

---

flee (FLEE): to run away from

Nothing but Water

Behind you, you hear a crashing sound. You want to look, but you're afraid to stop running.

Then it hits you. The speeding wave washes over you. It flips you around like a doll in a washing machine. You can see only water. You cannot breathe. The salt water stings your eyes. You struggle to keep your head above the angry water.

A Helping Hand

Suddenly, you see a hand. It is reaching toward you. A man is hanging on a tree trunk floating in the water. He is shouting at you.

You try to grab his hand. You grab it once, but can't hold on. Finally, he pulls you onto the tree trunk. You hold on as tightly as you can. The tree trunk twists in the rushing water.

Many areas remain under flood waters after a tsunami.

The 2004 tsunami left this mess in a street in Trincomalee, Sri Lanka.

Safe—For Now

The tree trunk is floating fast. Everywhere, people toss about in the water. Some are trying to swim. Others are not moving. Then, suddenly, you feel a change.

"What is it?" you ask yourself. It's the water! The wave is rushing back toward the ocean! Your tree trunk is being pulled back toward the sea. Luckily, the trunk jams up against a building. You stop moving.

Unforgettable

The wave is gone now. You look around. Everything is destroyed.

"Where is our town?" you ask the man.

He shakes his head. "It is gone."

This **tragedy** really happened. How? What can turn the ocean so deadly?

---

tragedy (TRAJ-uh-dee): a very sad event

The 2004 tsunami left streets in Banda Aceh, Indonesia, flooded.

CHAPTER 2

What Is a Tsunami?

A terrible tsunami struck the shores of the Indian Ocean in 2004. How did such a thing happen? What made this terrible wall of water?

Deep in the Ocean

The Indian Ocean tsunami began under the sea. A mighty **earthquake** shook the seafloor. A chunk of the seafloor shifted. This sudden movement made a great wave of water.

This great wave is called a *tsunami*. *Tsunami* is a Japanese word that means "**harbor** wave."

---

earthquake (URTH-kwayk): a sudden shaking of the earth
harbor (HAR-bur): a place where ships stay

The Earth Moves

The 2004 tsunami started near Sumatra
(soo-MAH-trah), a large island in the
Indian Ocean. Sumatra is part of the
country of Indonesia (in-doh-NEE-zhah)
in Southeast Asia.

Killer Waves

This tsunami moved very fast. It took only
15 minutes to reach Sumatra. It raced
toward Sri Lanka with a speed of 500 miles
(804 kilometers) an hour!

In a few hours, the tsunami also struck
Thailand, Sri Lanka, and India. Finally, it
reached Africa. The tsunami caused death
and **destruction**.

---

destruction (di-STRUHK-shun): when everything is
ruined and lost

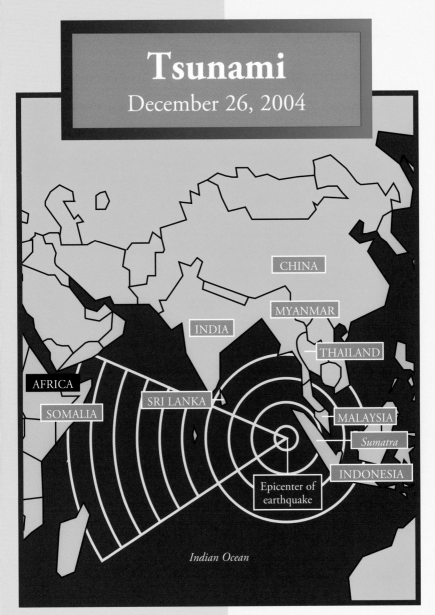

Tsunami
December 26, 2004

CHINA

MYANMAR

INDIA

THAILAND

AFRICA

SRI LANKA

SOMALIA

MALAYSIA

Sumatra

INDONESIA

Epicenter of
earthquake

Indian Ocean

*The light blue lines on this map
show the path of the tsunami.*

Many Causes of Tsunamis

An earthquake caused the Indian Ocean tsunami. But other events can cause tsunamis, too. An undersea **volcano** can cause a tsunami. So can **landslides** under the ocean.

---

volcano (vol-KAY-noh): a mountain through which melted rock, or lava, can flow

landslide (LAND-slide): the fast movement of rock and dirt

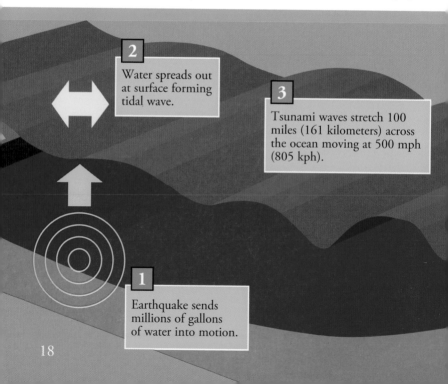

2 Water spreads out at surface forming tidal wave.

3 Tsunami waves stretch 100 miles (161 kilometers) across the ocean moving at 500 mph (805 kph).

1 Earthquake sends millions of gallons of water into motion.

Higher—and More Deadly!

In the open sea, the water is very deep. Here, tsunamis move very fast. But they are not high.

The water near the shore is **shallow**. In shallow water, tsunamis slow down. They grow much, much higher.

---

shallow (SHAL-oh): not deep

4 As waves reach shallow water, they slow down, which causes waves to grow higher.

5 Tsunami waves reach land, causing damage and destruction.

Can Animals Sense Tsunamis?

The 2004 tsunami hit Sri Lanka's largest national park. Thousands of people near the park died. But very few animals died. Why?

Scientists say animals can hear things people cannot hear. The animals likely heard the wave coming. They likely felt **vibrations** in the earth. The animals escaped to higher ground. Some snakes and lizards even climbed trees to escape the tsunami!

A herd of cows survived the 2004 tsunami.

vibration (vye-BRAY-shun): fast movement back and forth

A Deadly Force

Why can tsunamis cause such damage?
There are many reasons. They move so
fast and with such force that they surprise
people. People do not have time to escape.
Also, some buildings, bridges, and roads
are poorly made. Tsunamis can wash
them away.

Tsunamis can tear down power lines.
This can start fires. Tsunamis can break
open storage tanks and cause oil or other
unsafe matter to leak out. Floating cars
and trains can smash into things in
tsunami waves.

The 2004 Indian Ocean tsunami did
a great deal of harm. But other tsunamis
have also caused **misery**. You will learn
about a few in the next chapter.

---

misery (MIZ-ur-ee): discomfort or unhappiness

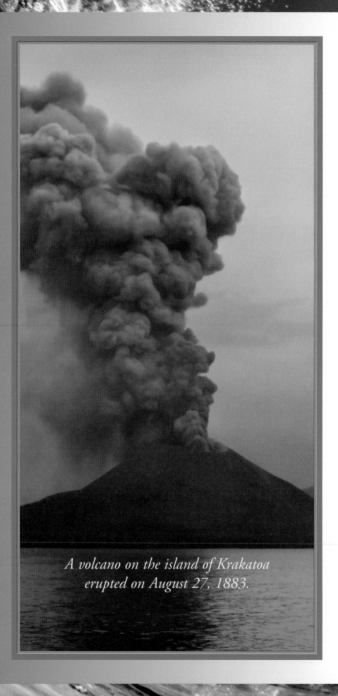

A volcano on the island of Krakatoa erupted on August 27, 1883.

— CHAPTER 3 —

Tsunamis of the Past

The lands in and around the Pacific Ocean have more volcanoes and earthquakes than any other place. Scientists have a name for these lands: the Ring of Fire!

The Biggest Boom!

What is the loudest sound ever heard? Many scientists think it was from a volcano **erupting** on Krakatoa (krak-uh-TOH-uh), an island in Indonesia.

People heard the eruption in Australia, 2,000 miles (3,219 kilometers) away! That's like someone in Boston hearing a sound made in Denver!

The volcano crashed into the sea. The splash created a huge tsunami.

---

erupt (i-RUHPT): to burst forth suddenly

Earthquakes and Tsunamis Around the Ring of Fire

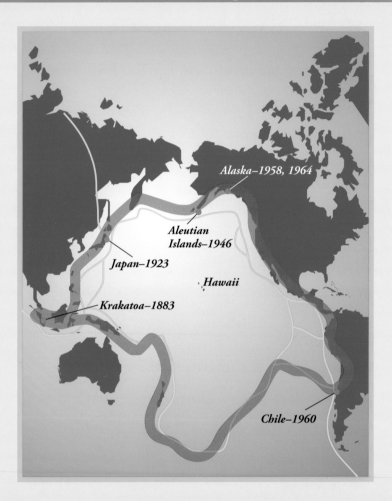

Alaska–1958, 1964

Aleutian Islands–1946

Japan–1923

Hawaii

Krakatoa–1883

Chile–1960

The yellow line shows some of the plates in the Earth's crust.
The red line shows the Ring of Fire. You can see how the
Ring of Fire follows the path of the plates.

Around the Ring of Fire

In 1923, a powerful earthquake hit Tokyo, Japan. The earthquake killed 140,000 people and caused a huge tsunami.

The strongest earthquake in the past 100 years happened off the coast of Chile. This earthquake in 1960 caused a great tsunami. The tsunami killed thousands of people in Chile. It also reached Hawaii, where 61 people died. The wave even killed 200 people in Japan. That's more than 10,440 miles (16,800 kilometers) away from Chile!

How Tall Was It?

How tall can a tsunami get? An earthquake in 1958 caused a rock slide in Lituya Bay, Alaska. The splash created a wave 1,720 feet (524 meters) high. That is 267 feet (81 meters) taller than the Empire State Building!

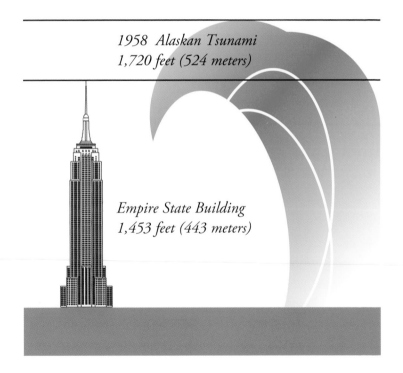

1958 Alaskan Tsunami
1,720 feet (524 meters)

Empire State Building
1,453 feet (443 meters)

Look Out, Alaska!

Many large tsunamis have happened in Alaska. One in 1946 was so tall it knocked over a lighthouse. In 1964, an earthquake hit Alaska's southern coast. The quake caused a tsunami that did damage as far away as Hawaii and southern California.

After a Tsunami

When a tsunami hits, people are killed. Homes are destroyed. People need help. Who gives the help these people need?

Local people in Indonesia helped unload supplies from helicopters after the 2004 tsunami.

Chapter 4

The World to the Rescue

After the 2004 tsunami, people needed help.
Many had lost everything. They had no homes, no
jobs, no food, no family. Many felt they had no hope.
Imagine you have come to help. What can you do?

A Living Nightmare

You will never forget what you see. Misery is everywhere. Schools, hospitals, and other buildings are gone. Millions are homeless.

You can't believe the crowds. Empty hands reach out to you. Tired voices ask for food and water. Scared eyes beg for your help.

A Terrible Cost

Then there are the dead. The killer wave took more than 200,000 lives. Thousands were buried. Many will never be found.

Doctors tell you about their greatest fear—sickness. Without **medicine**, toilets, clean water, and food, many will get sick. "How many more people could die?" you ask. "Thousands," answer the doctors.

Families were torn apart by the 2004 tsunami. These women pray at a grave site where victims are buried.

---

medicine (MED-uh-suhn): a drug or other substance used to treat an illness or injury

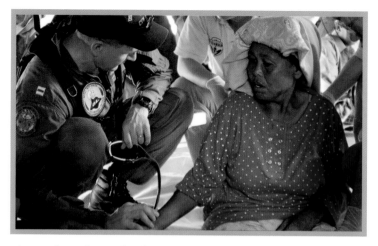

A member of a medical team from the U.S. Navy examines a patient in Indonesia.

Hope for the Future?

After the 2004 tsunami, there was much to do. People needed homes. Fishermen needed boats. Workers needed jobs and places to work. People needed to find missing friends and relatives.

The deadly wall of water brought a great cry for help. That cry was heard around the world. As the water returned to the sea, a wave of **charity** and kindness flowed in.

---

charity (CHA-ruh-tee): help given to others

Former U.S. presidents Bill Clinton and George H. W. Bush land in Sri Lanka to help the 2004 tsunami relief efforts.

Who Helps the Victims?

Many different groups helped the 2004 tsunami victims. Governments from around the world sent food, medicine, water, tools, and building supplies. The United Nations also gave aid.

Private Groups Lend a Hand

Private groups also helped. The **International** Red Cross gave medical aid. So did CARE and Save the Children. Doctors Without Borders rolled up their sleeves to help. OxFam gave food. Groups run by churches did their part.

All these groups share one thing. They get their money from everyday people like you!

---

private (PRYE-vit): not related to the government
international (in-tur-NASH-uh-nuhl): having to do with more than one country

Class Trips and Hot Chocolate

Young people everywhere helped after the 2004 tsunami. An eighth-grade class in Washington state was saving for a class trip. They gave their money to the Red Cross. Kids in chilly Michigan sold hot chocolate. In North Carolina, kids sold glasses of lemonade.

A boy in Atlanta held a bake sale with friends. The sale earned more than $100 for young tsunami victims. "I feel much better that I'm doing something to help those kids," the boy said.

Why No Warning?

The tsunami victims had no warning. Why? Isn't there some way to let people know that a tsunami is coming?

These children are selling lemonade outside their home.

This scientist studies tsunamis at the National Weather Service Pacific Tsunami Warning Center.

CHAPTER 5

Studying Tsunamis

Stuart Weinstein works at the Pacific Tsunami Warning Center in Hawaii. His job is to warn countries around the Pacific Ocean about tsunamis. On December 26, 2004, Weinstein saw something.

A Scientist at Work

Stuart Weinstein saw a change in his **instruments**. They told him there had been a strong earthquake in the Indian Ocean. Underwater earthquakes can cause tsunamis. Tsunamis in the Indian Ocean are uncommon. Weinstein told his boss, Charles McCreery. Together they studied the **data**.

---

instrument (IN-struh-muhnt): a tool for scientific work
data (DAY-tuh): information

Send Out a Warning!

McCreery decided to send out a warning. This message quickly went around the world. It told about the earthquake. It warned that a tsunami could occur in the Indian Ocean. But it was too late. The tsunami hit before anyone could reach safety.

National Weather Service Tsunami Warning Centers

Tsunami Warning Center, Palmer, Alaska

Tsunami Warning Center, Ewa Beach, Hawaii

Working Together

McCreery and Weinstein work at an international warning center in Hawaii. Another warning center is in Alaska. Both centers are part of the U.S. National Weather Service (NWS). The centers help protect people in the Pacific Ocean **region** from tsunamis.

No Warning

But the Indian Ocean has no tsunami warning centers. Why? Because tsunamis don't often happen there. Countries in the area spend money on warning systems for more common events such as tornadoes and floods. Now these countries are building tsunami warning systems as well.

---

region (REE-juhn): area

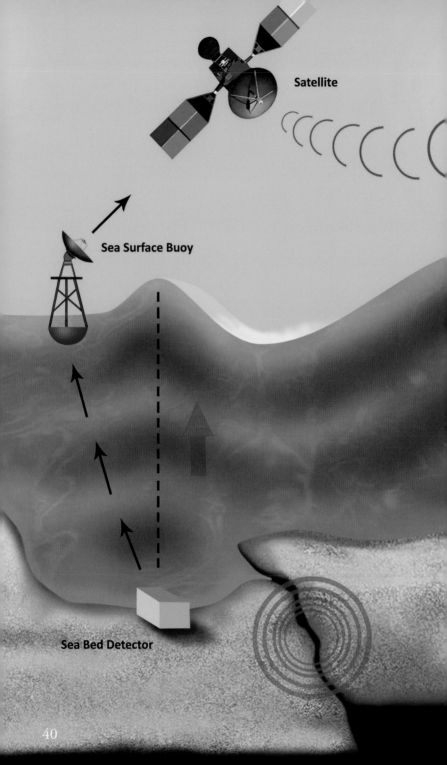

Satellite

Sea Surface Buoy

Sea Bed Detector

How Does a Warning System Work?

A warning system is made of several parts. These include **sensors**, **buoys**, and **satellites**.

Some sensors sit on the ocean floor. These might report earthquakes or water pressure changes. A change in water pressure might mean a tsunami is going by. The sensors send this data to buoys. The buoys send it to satellites. The satellites send it to scientists to study.

Forces of Nature

Tsunamis are a powerful force of nature. Some, like the 2004 tsunami, do great harm. The better we understand them, the less we need to fear them.

---

sensor (SEN-sur): an instrument that measures change
buoy (BOO-ee): an object floating in water held in place by an anchor
satellite (SAT-uh-lite): a spacecraft sent into orbit around Earth, another planet, or some object in space

Epilogue

Tsunami Facts

- Tsunamis can strike any low coastal area.

- Tsunamis can occur at any time.

- Tsunamis can travel up rivers and streams that lead to the ocean.

- Tsunamis move faster than you can run.

- Tsunamis are a series of waves.

The 2004 tsunami has made people understand how harmful these waves can be.

Staying Safe

If a tsunami strikes, here is what to do.

- Remember that tsunamis can have several waves. The first one is often not the largest.

- Stay away from all low-lying areas.

- Move to higher ground right away.

- Go to official tsunami safety areas.

- Follow the orders of emergency workers, teachers, and other trained adults.

Glossary

buoy (BOO-ee): an object floating in water held in place by an anchor

charity (CHA-ruh-tee): help given to others

data (DAY-tuh): information

destruction (di-STRUHK-shun): when everything is ruined and lost

earthquake (URTH-kwayk): a sudden shaking of the earth

erupt (i-RUHPT): to burst forth suddenly

flee (FLEE): to run away from

harbor (HAR-bur): a place where ships stay

instrument (IN-struh-muhnt): a tool for scientific work

international (in-tur-NASH-uh-nuhl): having to do with more than one country

landslide (LAND-slide): the fast movement of rock and dirt

medicine (MED-uh-suhn): a drug or other substance used to treat an illness or injury

misery (MIZH-ur-ee): discomfort or unhappiness

private (PRYE-vit): not related to the government

region (REE-juhn): area

satellite (SAT-uh-lite): a spacecraft sent into orbit around Earth, another planet, or some object in space

sensor (SEN-sur): an instrument that measures change

shallow (SHAL-oh): not deep

tourist (TOOR-ist): someone who travels for pleasure

tragedy (TRAJ-uh-dee): a very sad event

vibration (vye-BRAY-shun): fast movement back and forth

volcano (vol-KAY-noh): a mountain through which melted rock, or lava, can flow

Bibliography

Hort, Leonard. *Ring of Fire.* Science Links. Philadelphia: Chelsea Clubhouse, 2003.

Kehret, Peg. *Escaping the Giant Wave.* New York: Simon and Schuster Books for Young Readers, 2003.

Sorenson, Margo. *Tsunami! Death Wave.* Cover-to-Cover Books. Logan, Iowa: Perfection Learning, 1997.

Thompson, Luke. *Tsunamis.* High Interest Books. New York: Children's Press, 2000.

Wade, Mary Dodson. *Tsunami: Monster Waves.* American Disasters. Berkeley Heights, N.J.: Enslow, 2002.